Feeling Fabulous

Sweet treats...

"Yoo-hoo, Minnie!"

Hooray!

Bunny Hugs

Buzzy Pals

"What a handsome fan!"

"Oh, how lovely!"

My Sweetie!

Fashion is fun!

Happy Feet

Happy Day!

Sweet Friends

Minnie stirs the soup.

© Disney

"Hello, little friend!"

Ah, shucks!

Mickey and Minnie are best friends.

Daydreaming

© Disney

"I just love stripes!"

She's so sweet!

Minnie dribbles the soccer ball.

"I'm ready to roll!"

© Disney

"My hat!"

Shake your tailfeathers!

Daisy is such a diva!